Planet Earth

KINGFISHER
LONDON & NEW YORK

Distributed in the U.S. by Macmillan, 175 Fifth Ave., New York, NY 10010

First published as *Kingfisher Young Knowledge: Planet Earth* in 2006
Additional material produced for Kingfisher by Discovery Books Ltd.

Library of Congress Cataloging-in-Publication data has been applied for.

ISBN: 978-0-7534-6604-9

Kingfisher books are available for special promotions and premiums.
For details contact: Special Markets Department, Macmillan, 175 Fifth Ave., New York, NY 10010.

For more information, please visit www.kingfisherbooks.com

Printed in China
1 3 5 7 9 8 6 4 2
1TR/0511/WKT/UG/140MA

Note to readers: the website addresses listed in this book are correct at the time of going to print. However, due to the ever-changing nature of the Internet, website addresses and content can change. Websites can contain links that are unsuitable for children. The publisher cannot be held responsible for changes in website addresses or content or for information obtained through a third party. We strongly advise that Internet searches be supervised by an adult.

Acknowledgments
The publisher would like to thank the following for permission to reproduce their material. Every care has been taken to trace copyright holders. However, if there have been unintentional omissions or failure to trace copyright holders, we apologize and will, if informed, endeavor to make corrections in any future edition.
b = bottom, *c* = center, *l* = left, *t* = top, *r* = right

Photographs: *cover* Shutterstock Images; 2–3 Photolibrary.com; 4–5 Corbis Clay Perry; 6 Getty Imagebank; 7 Getty Stone; 8*bl* Photolibrary.com; 8–9 Science Photo Library Roger Harris; 9*b* Photolibrary.com; 12*l* Corbis Rupak de Chowdhuri; 13*t* Photolibrary.com; 13*br* Getty Photodisc; 12–13 Science Photo Library Pekka Parvianen; 16–17 Getty Imagebank; 16*cr* Photolibrary.com; 18*bl* Corbis NASA; 18–19 Getty Stone; 20–21 Corbis Tom Bean; 21*br* Getty AFP Yoshikazu Tsuno; 22–21 Corbis R.T. Holcomb; 23*tr* Corbis Charles & Josette Lenars; 24–25 Photolibrary.com; 24*c* Corbis Galen Rowell; 25*tl* Getty Stone; 26*l* Corbis Michael Freeman; 26–27 Getty Imagebank; 27*t* Photolibrary.com; 29 Corbis Audrey Gibson; 30–31 Getty Imagebank; 30*b* Corbis Robert Weight; 31*tr* Arcticphoto; 32–33 Corbis Yann Arthus-Bertrand; 32*bl* Frank Lane Picture Agency Minden Pictures; 33*tl* Photolibrary.com; 34–35 Photolibrary.com; 34*tr* Frank Lane Picture Agency Minden Pictures; 34*b* Getty Taxi; 35*bl* Corbis Craig Tuttle; 36–37 Frank Lane Picture Agency Minden Pictures; 36*b* Getty Stone; 37*tr* Corbis Michael Yamashita; 38–39 Getty Digital Vision; 38*b* Getty Photodisc; 39*br* Corbis Tim Wright; 40–41 Getty Digital Vision; 40*bl* Getty Photodisc; 41*c* Getty Photodisc; 48*b* Shutterstock Images/Julien Grondin; 48*t* Shutterstock Images/Marino Bocelli; 49 Shutterstock Images/kkaplin; 52*l* Shutterstock Images/Dmitry Naumov; 52*r* Shutterstock Images/Joao Virissimo; 53 Shutterstock Images/Chee-Onn Leong; 56 Shutterstock Images/Eduardo Rivero

Commissioned photography on pages 42–47 by Andy Crawford
Project maker and photoshoot coordinator: Jo Connor
Thank you to models Alex Bandy, Alastair Carter, Tyler Gunning, and Lauren Signist

Planet Earth

Deborah Chancellor

KINGFISHER
NEW YORK

Contents

What is Earth?

Earth is a planet in space. It is one of eight planets that circle around the Sun in our solar system. Seen from space, Earth looks blue. This is because most of it is covered with oceans and seas.

Central America

The continents

The large areas of land are called continents. We can see the shape of the continents in photos taken from space. This continent is South America.

South America

The atmosphere

There is a blanket of gases around Earth called the atmosphere. White clouds swirl around in our planet's atmosphere.

atmosphere

Inside Earth

Earth is a rocky planet. It is divided into three main parts—the crust, the mantle, and the core. We live on the crust, which is a thin layer of solid rock. Not far under our feet, the rock is so hot that it is liquid.

crust

The crust
In some places under the sea, Earth's crust is only 4 miles (6 kilometers) thick. Under most of the land, the crust is about 22 miles (35 kilometers) thick.

The core

The core is the hottest part of Earth. At its center, temperatures can reach up to 9,000°F (5,000°C).

inner core

outer core

The mantle

The hot rock in Earth's mantle melts to become liquid. We can see molten rock when a volcano erupts.

The water cycle

The world's water is never used up. The Sun warms up seawater, turning it to water vapor. This vapor rises into the air and then comes down as rain. The rain then flows back to the sea. This is called the water cycle.

Sun heats seawater, making water vapor

water falls as rain

Water world

Most of the world's water is in the oceans. Only one percent of all the world's water moves around in the water cycle.

water falls as rain

water vapor rises to form clouds

water collects in rivers and flows to the sea

Rain

Water vapor in clouds falls to the ground as rain. Some places get a lot of rain. Mawsynram, in northern India, gets more than 36 feet (11 meters) of rain every year. It is the wettest place in the world.

Weather and climate

Weather happens when the air around us changes. Air can be moving or still, hot or cold, wet or dry, or a mixture of these things. Water has a big part to play in the weather. Without it, there would be no clouds, rain, or fog.

Tropical climate
The weather that a place usually gets over a long time is called the climate. Climates vary in different parts of the world. In tropical places, the climate is hot and steamy.

Desert climate

In deserts, the climate is dry. On average, deserts have less than 1 inch (2.5 centimeters) of rain in a year. If all the rain comes at once, there are floods.

Trapping heat

Pollution in the air may trap some of the Sun's heat and stop it from escaping back into space. As a result, climates all over the world may be changing and may become more extreme.

Clouds, rain, and snow

Clouds are made up of millions of tiny water droplets or ice crystals. Water droplets in clouds join together to make raindrops, and ice crystals combine to form snowflakes. Clouds come in many shapes and sizes.

Snow
Snowflakes usually melt on their way down to Earth. But if the air near the ground is freezing, we get snow.

Different clouds

Low stratus clouds can bring rain. Fluffy cumulus clouds are seen on sunny days. High, wispy cirrus clouds are made of ice.

cirrus cloud

cumulus cloud

Thunder clouds

Cumulonimbus clouds are the biggest clouds of all. Some are taller than Earth's highest mountain, Mount Everest! They bring heavy rain, thunder, and lightning.

stratus cloud

Wind

Wind is air that is moving around. It can be as gentle as a breeze or as rough as a gale. Wind is made when the Sun warms the air to make it rise upward. Cold air rushes in to fill the gap, making a wind blow.

When the wind blows

Wind travels at different speeds. A light breeze makes clouds drift across the sky. Stronger winds make trees sway, while very strong winds, called hurricanes, can cause a lot of damage.

Air currents

Birds can glide along on
rising currents of warm
air. Seagulls hardly need
to flap their wings at all
to stay high up in the sky.

Hurricanes and tornadoes

Hurricanes and tornadoes are dangerous wind storms. Hurricanes form over the sea, and when they reach land, they can cause terrible damage. Tornadoes are powerful whirlwinds that form over land.

Hurricane
This satellite photo shows a hurricane in the Caribbean Sea. It is heading for the coast of Florida.

Twister

Tornadoes are also called twisters. Wind speed at the center of a twister reaches up to 250 miles (400 kilometers) per hour—this is the fastest wind on Earth.

Earthquakes

An earthquake is a shaking or trembling of Earth's surface caused by forces underground. Most earthquakes are too weak to be noticed, but strong ones can crack the ground and cause houses to fall down.

Fault zones

Most earthquakes happen at fault zones, where the plates that make up Earth's crust push or slide against one another. This sends massive vibrations through the rock that shake the surface.

movement of plate

Fault line

This huge crack in the ground is the San Andreas Fault, in California. Two of Earth's plates grind past each other here. They have caused some massive earthquakes.

Earthquake drill

Earthquakes are quite common in some places. In Japan, schoolchildren wear protective hats when practicing what to do if there is an earthquake.

Volcanoes

A volcano is a mountain that was made from molten rock called lava. The lava comes from deep under the ground. During an eruption, it forces its way up through a weak point in Earth's crust. Volcanoes can erupt on land or deep under the ocean.

Inside a volcano

Molten rock, called magma, collects in a chamber. When the volcano erupts, magma is forced upward, through a vent.

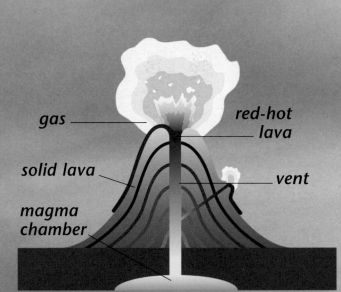

gas

red-hot lava

solid lava

vent

magma chamber

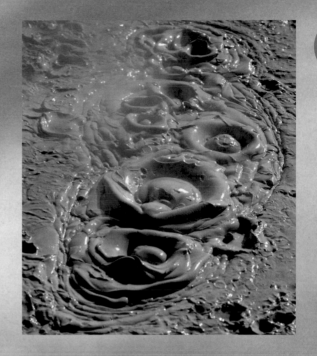

Bubbling mud

The land around volcanoes becomes very hot. Pools of mud or water bubble and boil on Earth's surface.

Giant volcano

The biggest active volcano in the world is in Hawaii. This lava flow is from the Mauna Ulu crater there.

Mountains

Mountains form over millions of years. They are made when two plates under Earth's crust push together, forcing up huge folds of rock. As the mountain is pushed upward, ice, wind, and weather wear it down. This is called erosion.

The Alps

The Alps in Europe are a few million years old. Young mountains have jagged peaks because the weather has not had time to smooth down the sharp edges of rock.

The Himalayas

The 14 tallest mountains in the world are in the Himalayas, in Asia. These mountains are more than 50 million years old.

Rivers and lakes

Most rivers carry water downhill to lakes or the sea. Some are so powerful they change the shape of the land they pass through. They carry rocks and mud along with them, cutting deep valleys and gorges as they go.

Lakes

Lakes are large areas of fresh water surrounded by land. Lakes are usually found in valley bottoms, but they sometimes form in the craters of old volcanoes (left).

A river's journey

A river begins its journey in high ground, where it flows quickly downhill. When a river reaches flat ground, it flows much more slowly and can sometimes form large bends called meanders.

Grand Canyon

The Colorado River has carved out the deepest gorge in the world. The fast-moving waters have worn away the rock to help create the amazing Grand Canyon.

The oceans

Oceans cover most of planet Earth. They are deeper in some places than in others. This is because the ocean floor is not flat. There are mountains, valleys, plains, and deep trenches under the sea.

Big blue sea

The five main oceans are the Arctic, Atlantic, Pacific, Indian, and Southern. The largest of these oceans is the Pacific.

volcano

shipwreck

deep trench

Low tide

At low tide, rockpools can be found on rocky beaches. The pools are covered over again at high tide.

Islands

Some underwater mountains and volcanoes are so tall that they rise above the surface of the water. Many islands are actually the tips of underwater mountains.

mountain range

island

The poles

The North Pole is in the middle of the Arctic Ocean. This is a frozen ocean, surrounded by the world's most northern lands. The South Pole is at the heart of Antarctica. Most of this continent is covered with thick ice.

Antarctic science

Antarctica is the coldest and windiest continent. The only people who live there are scientists, who work in research stations.

Icebergs

In Antarctica and the Arctic, icebergs break away from ice sheets or glaciers and float in the icy ocean. We see only a tiny part of an iceberg— the rest is hidden underwater.

Northern Lights

The Northern Lights, or aurora borealis, can be seen in northern Canada, Alaska, and Scandinavia. The spectacular display takes place high up in the atmosphere.

Deserts

Deserts are the driest places on Earth, because it hardly ever rains there. Some deserts are sandy, and others are rocky. Some are very hot, while others are freezing cold in the winter.

Desert plants

Cactus plants grow in American deserts. They can live for a long time without rain because they store water in their thick stems. Some birds make their homes in cactus stems.

Wind erosion

Deserts can be windy places. Wind blasts sand at tall rocks, gradually wearing them away. The rocks in Monument Valley, in the southwestern United States, show how wind can change the landscape in a desert.

Biggest desert

The Sahara, in northern Africa, is the biggest hot desert in the world. It contains the world's tallest sand dunes, which are up to 1,410 feet (430 meters) high and 3 miles (5 kilometers) long.

Forests

A forest is a large area of land covered in trees. About one-fifth of the world is covered with forests. In the past, forests grew over much more of the planet, but people have cut down many of the trees.

Deciduous
Trees that lose leaves in the winter are called deciduous. The leaves change color and drop from the trees in the fall.

Rainforest

Rainforests grow in hot countries where there is a lot of rain. The wettest rainforests have more than 33 feet (10 meters) of rainfall per year.

Evergreen

Big forests of evergreen trees grow in northern parts of the world. Evergreen trees do not lose their leaves in the winter. Their branches slope down, so the snow slides off them.

Life on Earth

Earth may be the only planet in the universe that can support life. Our planet's oxygen and the water in the oceans are vital for living things to survive.

Rainforest life

There are many millions of types, or species, of animals and plants on Earth. Tropical rainforests are home to more than half of the world's plant and animal species.

When life began

Scientists believe that life on Earth began more than 3.5 billion years ago. It has been slowly changing, or evolving, ever since. Remains of ancient creatures tell us a lot about life a very long time ago.

In the ocean

The oceans were home to the world's first animals. Some ocean species, such as sea turtles, are more than 200 million years old.

Earth's riches

Many of Earth's natural riches are hidden deep under the ground. Fossil fuels, such as oil and gas, are found in rocks thousands of feet below Earth's surface. They are made from the remains of ancient plants and animals.

Minerals

Rocks are made from minerals. Rare minerals, such as the diamonds and rubies in this crown, are called gems.

Oil and gas

Oil and gas are fossil fuels that are pumped up from holes drilled into Earth's crust. They are found in places that are, or once were, under the sea.

Coal

Coal is a fossil fuel that is burned in huge amounts to make electricity. It is dug out from deep underground mines.

Taking care of Earth

Earth gives us food, water, and air to breathe. Sadly, people have not taken care of it, and many places are now polluted. Many plants and animals have died out or soon will. We must all help make Earth a cleaner place.

Saving forests

Trees help keep the air clean and provide shelter for many different animals. People must stop cutting down so many forests and should plant more trees.

Recycling

We can make new things from old materials. This is called recycling. Bottles, cans, paper, plastic, and tinfoil can all be recycled.

New energy

Scientists are developing new forms of energy that do not pollute. Many of the forces of nature, such as the wind, can be used to make electricity.

Make a volcano

Understanding eruptions

There are about 1,500 active volcanoes in the world today. When a volcano erupts, huge underground pressures force liquid rock up into the air. You can make your own volcano with some simple materials. In your volcano, baking soda (sodium bicarbonate) mixes with vinegar to make carbon dioxide gas.

Using the clay, make a hollow volcano and place it on the tray. Slide the plastic bottle inside.

You will need:
- Modeling clay
- Baking tray
- Small plastic bottle with the top sliced off
- Baking soda
- Funnel
- Vinegar
- Red food coloring

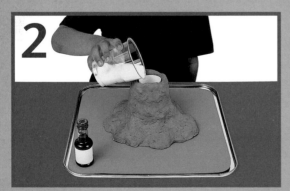

Fill the bottle halfway up with baking soda. You may need to use the funnel for this.

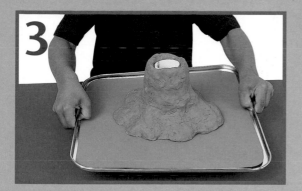

Place your volcano and baking tray on a flat surface. You can take it outside if you prefer.

Mix the vinegar with the food coloring. Pour them into the bottle using the funnel.

Stand back and watch your volcano erupt!

Make a rain gauge

Measuring rain

There is an easy way to measure how much rain falls during a rain shower. Put your rain gauge out in the open. When the shower is over, open the lid and collect the rain water in a measuring jug. Write down how much rain fell.

You will need:
- Large plastic bottle
- Scissors
- Rubber bands
- Garden pole or stick
- Measuring jug
- Pen and paper

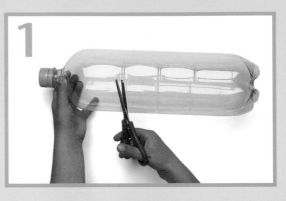

Cut a section off the plastic bottle, using the scissors. You may need to ask an adult to help you.

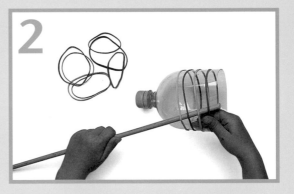

Put rubber bands around the bottle. Slide the pole under the bands and position the bottle with the screw cap facing down, to catch any raindrops.

Make a windmill

Spinning sails

You cannot see the wind, but you can watch what it does. Make a windmill and see how the wind blows it around.

You will need:
- 2 squares of colored cardboard
- Pencil and ruler
- Scissors and tape
- Thumbtacks and wooden rod

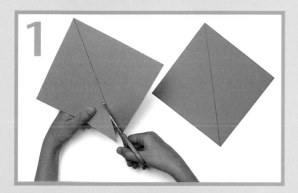

1 Draw a line across each cardboard square, from one corner to the other. Cut along this line to make two triangles.

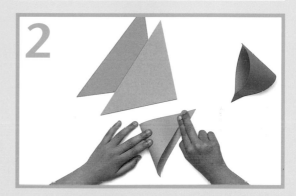

2 You will now have four triangles. Fold each of the triangles in half, taping the corners together.

3 Place the corners of the four triangles on top of one another. Ask an adult to help you pin them onto the wooden rod.

Forest habitat

Make your own forest

The place in which an animal lives is called a habitat. Everything an animal needs in order to survive can be found in its habitat—for example, food and shelter. There are many different types of animal habitats on Earth. You can make a model of a forest habitat with craft supplies.

tree template to draw around

You will need:

- Big shoebox
- Poster paints and paintbrush
- Pencil
- Tracing paper
- Cardboard
- Scissors
- Glue
- Modeling clay
- Plant material—leaves, grass, or twigs
- Toy forest animals

Paint inside your shoebox, using brown paint for the ground, green for the grass, and blue for the sky.

Use the template on the opposite page to draw some trees on the cardboard. Cut out the plant shapes.

Paint the trees. When they are dry, attach them inside the box with glue or clay. Scatter the plant material on the ground and arrange your animals in their new home.

Glossary

atmosphere—the air around Earth

cactus—a plant that can grow in places with little rain

crust—the layer of rock around Earth

currents—movements of air or water in a particular direction

drill—a repeated practice or exercise

droplets—very small drops of liquid

eruption—the pouring out of hot, molten rock from a volcano

fault—a break in Earth's crust

gas—a substance that is not a solid or a liquid. Air is a mixture of gases

glaciers—moving rivers of ice

gorges—valleys with steep sides

ice crystals—tiny pieces of ice

magma—molten rock underground

mineral—a hard natural substance that makes up rocks

oxygen—one of the gases in the air

plates—Earth's crust is made up of about 12 large plates

polluted—made dirty by waste substances

pollution—harmful waste that damages the environment

rainforest—a dense forest of tall trees that grows in a tropical area

sand dunes—big hills of sand that are formed by the wind

satellite photo—a photograph taken from a satellite orbiting Earth

solar system—the planets that orbit the Sun

trenches—long, narrow valleys

tropical—belonging to the tropics—an area around the equator with hot, wet weather

valleys—areas of low land between hills or mountains

vapor—a mass of tiny water droplets in the air

whirlwind—a strong wind in a tight spiral

The content of this book will be useful to help teach and reinforce various elements of the science and language arts curricula in the elementary grades. It also provides opportunities for crosscurricular lessons in geography, art, and mapping.

Extension activities:

Writing
Picture yourself on the raft on p. 27. Write down the dialog between you and the others on the raft as you hurtle down the river at full speed!

You are a tiny drop of water in a river rushing toward the sea. You stop in a lake where—oops!—you evaporate in the sunlight and rise to become part of a cloud. Write the rest of this adventure story, telling about all the places you visit as you travel through the water cycle.

What can YOU do to help take care of Earth? Make a list of at least five different things that you and your friends could do to help. Then start with one and do it!

Science
The topic of planet Earth relates to the scientific themes of the structure of Earth, forces of Earth, weather and climate, and changes in Earth and the sky.

Some specific links to science curriculum content include biomes and ecosystems (pp. 24–35); human impact (pp. 38–41); evolution (pp. 36–37); resources (pp. 38–41); properties, locations, movement of objects in the sky (pp. 6–7); weathering (pp. 24–25); water cycle (pp. 10–11, 14–15); solar system (pp. 6–7); and natural hazards (pp. 18–23).

Crosscurricular links
Writing, oral language, and art
Choose one of the ecosystems described on pp. 24–35. Research to learn more about its particular characteristics. Write a short report, including drawings of several of its typical plants and animals. Give a three-to-five-minute presentation of your work.

Oral language and art
Using the information on pp. 10–11 or another source, draw a large diagram of the water cycle. Label all the parts. Give a three-minute presentation explaining how the water cycle works.

Geography
List the names of the different environments featured on pp. 30–35. (Note: there are three described on pp. 34–35.) Research to find where in the world examples of these different environments are located and find them on a world map.

Writing, art, and mapping
The bird in the picture on p. 32 has pecked a hole through the cactus to make a home inside. What would it be like to live inside a giant cactus? Write a story describing your cactus house. Include a diagram of your floor plan and pictures showing different views of the inside of your home.

Using the projects
Children can do these projects at home. Here are some ideas for extending them:

Pages 42–43: After you have gotten your model volcano to work, ask if you can demonstrate it to younger children. Be sure that your explanation includes telling what happens when a real volcano erupts.

Page 44: Continue to use your rain gauge every day for a month or more. Use a small notebook to keep a careful record of the rainfall for each day. Make a bar or line graph to show the rainfall for the month.

Page 45: Make several identical windmills. Put them outside facing in different directions and watch how the wind (and changes in the wind) affect each one.

Pages 46–47: The forest shown in this activity is a deciduous forest (see p. 34). Make a second display showing a rainforest or evergreen forest. Look for similarities and differences.

Did you know?

- Earth is more than 4.5 billion years old.

- Seventy percent of Earth's surface is covered in water.

- The largest recorded earthquake in the world was in Chile on May 22, 1960. It measured 9.5 on the Richter scale.

- The world's longest mountain range is the Andes in South America. It stretches 4,475 miles (7,200 kilometers), north to south.

- More than 16 million thunderstorms take place around the world each year.

- The largest cactus in the world is the saguaro cactus. Some cacti have been known to reach 46 feet (14 meters) in height.

- The highest mountain in the world is Mount Everest in the Himalayas. It is 29,035 feet (8,850 meters) tall.

- Earth's crust varies in thickness under land, but it is generally between 20 and 30 miles (30–50 kilometers) thick.

- The longest river in the world is the Nile, in Africa. It is 4,132 miles (6,650 kilometers) long.

- Antarctica is the coldest place on Earth. Temperatures as low as −128°F (−89°C) have been recorded.

- One in ten of the known animal species in the world live in the Amazon rainforest.

- There are at least 1,500 active volcanoes around the world.

- The Californian redwood is the tallest species of tree in the world. It can grow to more than 330 feet (100 meters) tall.

- The driest place on Earth is Arica, Chile, where as little as 0.03 inches (0.76 millimeters) of rain falls in a year.

- The world's largest ocean is the Pacific, covering 65.3 million square miles (169.2 million square kilometers).

- Earth is 7,926 miles (12,756 kilometers) in diameter.

- The Grand Canyon (below) is the largest canyon on Earth, reaching a depth of more than 1.1 miles (1.8 kilometers).

Planet Earth quiz

The answers to these questions can all be found by looking back through the book. See how many you get right. You can check your answers on page 56.

1) Where can the world's biggest active volcano be found?
   A—Holland
   B—Hawaii
   C—Haiti

2) What is underground molten rock called?
   A—magma
   B—lava
   C—crust

3) How hot can Earth's core get?
   A—1,800°F (1,000°C)
   B—5,400°F (3,000°C)
   C—9,000°F (5,000°C)

4) What are trees that lose their leaves in the winter called?
   A—deciduous
   B—conifers
   C—evergreen

5) What are the gases that form a blanket around Earth called?
   A—clouds
   B—the atmosphere
   C—the solar system

6) How old are the Himalayan Mountains?
   A—50 million years
   B—50,000 years
   C—500 years

7) Which of these deserts is the largest hot desert on Earth?
   A—the Gobi Desert
   B—the Sahara Desert
   C—the Arabian Desert

8) Where are hurricanes formed?
   A—over the ocean
   B—over mountains
   C—over the desert

9) What speed can the wind at the center of a tornado reach?
   A—25 miles (40km) per hour
   B—250 miles (400km) per hour
   C—2,500 miles (4,000km) per hour

10) Who are the only people that live in Antarctica?
    A—astronomers
    B—miners
    C—scientists

11) What percentage of the world's water moves around in the water cycle?
    A—1 percent
    B—10 percent
    C—100 percent

12) When do scientists believe that life on Earth began?
    A—3,500 years ago
    B—3.5 million years ago
    C—3.5 billion years ago

Books to read

Explorers: Planet Earth by Dan Gilpin, Kingfisher, 2011

Flip the Flaps Planet Earth by Mike Goldsmith, Kingfisher, 2010

Guide to the Planet (Planet Earth) by Steve Murrie and Matthew Murrie, Scholastic Inc., 2009

The World's Oceans (Amazing Planet Earth) by Jen Green, Franklin Watts, 2009

Navigators: Planet Earth by Barbara Taylor, Kingfisher, 2009

Earth's Water Cycle (Planet Earth) by Amy Bauman, Gareth Stevens Publishing, 2008

Places to visit

Rainforests of the World, California Academy of Sciences, San Francisco, California
www.calacademy.org/academy/exhibits/rainforest/
Explore the wonders of a rainforest contained in the museum's four-story dome—including colorful chameleons, croaking frogs, and a busy Bornean bat cave. Watch birds and butterflies flying among the treetops and descend in a glass elevator to a flooded forest floor.

The Discovery Center, Boston, Massachusetts
www.mos.org/discoverycenter/
Experience being a real scientist at the Discovery Center. Visitors can pretend to be a geologist at the Geology Field Station or work as a marine biologist on the Coral Reef Boat.

The Hall of Biodiversity, American Museum of Natural History, New York
www.amnh.org/exhibitions/permanent/biodiversity/
The Hall of Biodiversity exhibition is devoted to the need to protect the planet's biodiversity. The Spectrum of Life exhibit takes visitors through the incredible story of evolution and Earth's amazing diversity.

Websites

NASA Science
http://kids.earth.nasa.gov/
NASA's Earth Science projects are related to Earth's crust, tropical rainfall, thunderstorms, and water. Find out how you can get involved in these exciting Earth Science programs and projects!

Forests, Deserts, and Wetlands Facts
http://idahoptv.org/dialogue4kids/season8/forestsdesertswetlands/facts.cfm
A site packed full of information and facts about forests, deserts, and wetlands, with specific reference to those found in the state of Idaho.

Cool Facts about Antarctica
www.highlightskids.com/Science/Postcards/h1polarFacts.asp
How cold is it in Antarctica? When was Antarctica discovered? Who owns it, and who lives there? Find out some truly cool facts at this site.

Planet Earth
quiz answers

1) B	7) B
2) A	8) A
3) C	9) B
4) A	10) C
5) B	11) A
6) A	12) C